Moving beyond Mind

Moving beyond Mind

Kyle P. Harper

www.kylepharper.com

ISBN-10: 0983403929

ISBN-13: 978-0-9834039-2-0

Dedication

This book is dedicated to all of those in search of the Truth, especially my mother, Brenda Jones, who sparked this supreme desire in me.

Contents

Acknowledgements

Sara, Avery and Eli for providing daily living examples of unconditional love.

Thank you. I love you.

Introduction

On February 16, 2011, I had an indescribable experience. I only point toward it by saying it was a nonphysical orgasm spawned by the connection of my soul to the cosmic soul. In this total connection, I became the Universe and everything in it. I became one with God. I became God. Not a God that is separate from me, but the God that is me at my core–the God that is at the core of all of humanity.

Upon having this experience, I felt compelled to try to capture what had just happened in words. Although words fail to describe, they are brush strokes creating an interpretation of the ecstasy when joining as The Whole. This attempt to describe the indescribable was the first of the writings that make up *Moving beyond Mind*.

Awakening, I continued to be given ideas from the nonlocal. Coming to me as feelings and energy, I translated into words. As I wrote, I felt as if the messages were being handed down as instructions for my own life. I wrote them without hesitation or suppression, for I was the only one in the audience. It was only later I decided to share them.

I share them hoping they will help you, if in no other way than providing motivation for you to search within yourself for truth.

All of us have the power to tap into the infinite–creation and evolution–God. Really, it is not even tapping into it: it is just removing the cap we have placed over the source. All we have to do is allow it to flow through us. So often we are so busy "trying," we find it harder to let go and go with the flow than to continue our struggle. Yet our struggle is what causes our struggle. Life is easier if we just let go of judgment and ride the wave of love. *Moving beyond Mind* is my attempt to get out of my own way and let the energy of life flow through me without constriction.

Tap the well that is inside you and let it flow.

Love,
Kyle

Moving beyond Mind

2.16.2011
I am God ...

1

I am God, a face in the clouds.

Not a face in the earthly clouds we so often see depicted, but a face in the cosmic cloud. The cosmic dust cloud at the extreme tip of the Universe as it speeds to expansion. Evolution's force drives me forward on the whitewater rush of the cosmic wave.

 I laugh in bliss and then shriek in ecstasy as the neck of my earth body arches back and my face turns up, mouth gaping in awe, toward the earthly heavens that contain my material self; while my real self, my God being, surfs the fantastic rush of a cosmic tsunami expanding exponentially faster into the void of pure potential.

I giggle in child-like fashion as I am swallowed by the bliss of total Unity.

Instantly, my mind torques the vice of thought, squeezing the gap in which I swim, until the bubble pops. The raging river of worldly thought devours my dam of blissful peace, and I wonder, as I sit beside the pond at the park, what the ladies walking by me think of my facial expressions.

I am back … on the surface of existence.

2.18.2011

How deceived we are …

2

How deceived we are by what our eyes see, by what our mind leads us to believe *is* us.

We are not the body;
We are not the mind;
We are the energy.
We are the flow.

We are not the body, we are the consciousness that gives the body life.
We are not the mind, we are the observer of thought.
We are not the flower, we are the opening of the bloom.
We are not the tree, we are the growth from the seed.
We are not the earth, we are the force that turns it.
We are not the universe, we are the expansion of it.

We are, then, the One that unites all things.

2.21.2011

Sexual energy is the energy of God ...

3

Sexual energy is the energy of God, of Creation.
We are each created out of this magnificent energy—the energy of life.

Just as we are much more than our physical body, sex energy is much
    more than its physical expression.
Embrace sexual energy for what it is: the most potent energy
    of evolution.
Direct it toward higher places.
It will expand your consciousness.

Move it to the heart for love and compassion,
Move it to the throat for creativity,
Move it to the third eye for clarity,
Move it to the crown for enlightenment!

Live, love and grow in the energy of life.

2.22.2011

Everything you see ...

4

Everything you see around you was created by you.
You have created everything in your environment.
All the details are your choosing.
The world around you is a reflection of your inner world: your
thoughts, your feelings.
You have complete control.
You can continue down the current path or you can change at
any moment.
You have complete freedom.

2.23.2011
Clarity … is the only goal …

5

Clarity, to see things as they are, is the only goal. Believe this thought and ask for clarity.

2.23.2011

Creation is love, bliss and happiness …

6

Creation is love, bliss and happiness.
When you are the creative being that is your essence, you
    experience bliss.
When you are love, you experience bliss.
When you are one with the force of evolution, you experience bliss.
Meditate. Love. Create.

2.23.2011

Love expands from your heart …

7

Love expands from your heart to the edge of the universe and beyond.
You are love.
Feel the expansiveness.

2.24.2011

The second coming of Christ …

8

The second coming of Christ is not some far off event that will happen
    out there;
It is happening right now in you.
It is the awakening:
The awakening to love,
The awakening to your true self.
Share your message with the world;
Now is the time.
Christ is not coming to us but through us!

2.24.2011

You have the potential …

9

You have the potential to have two types of thoughts: ego thoughts and God thoughts.

Ego thoughts are a rehash of our past. They are the replaying of our past or the projecting of our past into the future. Don't be deceived–thoughts of the future are not new thoughts. They are thoughts gathered from our past and projected into the future from the perspective of our past. How can we know anything other than what we have experienced?

God thoughts originate in the collective consciousness. They are the thoughts of Evolution. They circulate in the energy that flows through the body. The energy is the true self. You must create space in between the ego's thoughts so that your mind can pick up God's thoughts flowing through you. You must witness your thoughts so you hear God speak.

How do you know if you are experiencing your true thoughts, God's thoughts, or the ego's thoughts? By your feeling. The ego's thoughts create fear, doubt, anger and anxiety. Your true thoughts create love.

2.28.2011

Evolutionary force is the seed of all desires …

10

Evolutionary force is the seed of all desires. The Universe and all things in it are evolving. This is the purpose of existence, to evolve. Your desires all stem from the calling of evolution. Just as the universe desires to be ever improving, so do you. The mistake that you make is the confusion of how to fulfill your desire to evolve and improve.

You think the desire to be better is a desire for betterment on the outside, to have more and better things around you. This is confusion. The evolutionary desire, therefore, your true desire, is to evolve on the inside by expanding your consciousness. By evolving your consciousness, you change how you view the world, and you are happy. In fact, you are your happiest. You can only be totally fulfilled when you are expanding your consciousness. This is you waking up to your relationship with the Universe.

When you consciously join in unity with that which is you, everything and every force in the Universe conspire to help you fulfill your desires.

3.1.2011

Your thoughts, emotions and feelings control …

11

Your thoughts, emotions and feelings control your internal, and therefore, your external world. A situation that takes place in your environment cannot affect you personally unless you invite it in and nurture it. An event cannot cause stress. You cause stress by your reaction to the event. You are choosing to create stress. If you are currently in a reactive state of being, that is, you are not aware, then you will argue with this statement. If you have started to awaken, you will feel its truth. You have the power to control everything inside of you. You control your own level of stress or happiness, not your environment. It is your perception that combines your thoughts with emotions and produces feelings.

3.3.2011

Beauty is in the flow ...

12

Beauty is in the flow.

The unfolding of the flower,
The rush of the stream,
The dance of light.

Objects, which at first glance are overlooked as boring, ooze with
   appeal when their true state, the state of motion, is seen.
Everything in the Universe is in motion, flowing, at every moment.

Open your eyes to the flow, and beauty will surround you.

3.4.2011

Happiness is a perspective ...

13

Happiness is a perspective: clarity without noise, action without fear.

3.7.2011

The time has come …

14

The time has come for you to join and become one, both internally and externally. You have become divided, and you have lost your strength. The ego must be put aside. You have the ability to make life joyous for all. All that is necessary is for you to make life joyful for yourself. Once you are truly happy, then you can spread the joy of happiness. Until that time, you must focus on yourself. You must focus on becoming One.

3.8.2011

Enlightenment is realizing …

15

Enlightenment is realizing that you are doing exactly what you are supposed to be doing.

3.9.2011

The secret to greatness ...

16

The secret to greatness is to be exactly who you are without dumbing yourself down to meet the expectations of society.

3.10.2011

Peace is of primary importance …

17

Peace is of primary importance to society right now. We must see past our differences by realizing that we are no different at all. Our differences are rooted in fear, the fear our ego projects. We live in an abundant world. We are all human, and our deepest desires are very similar. We are much more similar than different even in our currently fragmented state. We must awaken to our Oneness. Heaven and hell are not geographic locations but outcomes of our chosen evolutionary path. We have been given a world that is inherently heaven. We are currently on a path to make it hell. We are free to choose our own destiny.

3.11.2011

The whole universe has conspired ...

18

The whole universe has conspired since the beginning of time to bring you this exact moment. Accept it for what it is, a miraculous symphony of events riding the force of evolution, and be grateful.

3.16.2011
The perception of comfort ...

19

The perception of comfort is just that. To be truly comfortable we must know our own nature, who we are at our core. Not who we are on the surface, but deep down in the aquifers of our consciousness. True happiness comes from knowing our unique self, not trying to adopt another's image for our own.

One must look deep within for bliss. Once it is tapped, it will flow through you like water from the well.

3.24.2011

God is intelligence, the force of the universe ...

20

God is intelligence, the force of the universe, evolution. We are the manifestation of God.

3.29.2011

We have the ability to tap into an intelligence ...

21

We have the ability to tap into an intelligence far greater than our own intellect. A collective intelligence that ties all of us together. Think of the vast intelligence that rules our Universe. The planet rotates so that the sun rises every morning exactly on time. Birds fly south for the winter thousands of miles and return to the exact spot in the spring. Salmon return to their birth place to lay eggs. These animals have small intellectual capacity compared with humans, and yet they seem to have more intelligence in these circumstances than we. We as humans are currently living too much from our individual intellect and too little from the universal intelligence we all share.

3.30.2011

There is essentially no difference …

22

There is essentially no difference in believing in God and not believing in God. They are both incomplete views. If you believe in God, then you have a limited view of God. You see God as an entity separate from yourself. You have not experienced God; therefore, you must believe. If you don't believe in God, it is probably because of the limited view of God that society holds. You have been pushed into believing there is an old man sitting on a cloud in the sky waiting to punish you when you do wrong. You have rejected this idea because you know in your heart that this is simply not true.

Saying that you believe in God is like saying that you believe in the Sun. Do you believe in the Sun? Of course not! The statement doesn't make sense. The Sun is. You know it is there; you do not have to believe in it. The same holds true with God. You either realize God or you don't: it has nothing to do with belief.

You cannot find the whole by separating. You cannot find love while persuading. Love is acceptance. Love is Unity.

If one truly does know God, then one knows that God is · everywhere and everything. I am God, you are God, the flowers are God–everything is made up of God. If you do not agree with the terminology, then you can use energy. Science saying that everything is energy and you saying everything is God are the same things, just different words. A scientist saying the universe is intelligent and you saying that God is all knowing are again the same things. God is the force of creation, the force of evolution, the intelligence of the universe–love. God is everywhere, and when you connect to the Unity, you become everywhere and everything. You become God, and you disappear. Then as God, when you look for God, you only find emptiness. You are what you seek.

3.31.2011

The hole we seek to fill …

23

The hole we seek to fill
The craving unsatisfied
The joy not embraced
The love we justify

The life we forget to live
The consciousness wasted
Our eyes see thoughts and weep
Our hearts ache from separation
Our soul buried deep
The mind reins our kingdom
How do we awaken
And finally know freedom

What we seek is within
Our craving – to know
Joy comes from love
Life awakens and unfolds
Consciousness opens our eyes
There is no separation

Our souls dance
We Unite
One we are in the light

We are not separate
We're the whole
Freed from the ego
Embodying the soul

4.4.2011

After 36 years ...

24

After 36 years, I saw for the first time the flowering of a dogwood tree.
After 36 years, I saw for the first time the rays of the Sun kissing
    my cheek.
After 36 years, I saw for the first time the dance of pines swaying in
    the breeze.
After 36 years, the fog has lifted, and the light shines bright in my eyes.

4.7.2011

The warm emptiness ...

25

The warm emptiness of an adolescent love affair blossoming in the
spring air fills my stomach.
The deep comfort of a loving parent's gentle embrace during a
childhood crisis overtakes my being.
Energy flows from my core out to and beyond the surface of my body
as my billions of cells dance to the music of life.

I am an infant babbling in bliss, verbalizing the perfect oneness of
the womb,
I am the child with no fear, knowing that the world offers no problem
mother can't fix,
I am the teenager tingling, anticipating the sweet sensations of
embracing my lover,
I am the young adult whose eyes twinkle with delight feeling her soul
merge with "the one,"
I am the new parent hearing the eternal silence that fills the room
before the exhale of life's first breath,
I am the student clearing the fog of my past–opening myself to
evolutionary intelligence,
I am the teacher receiving the gratitude of a lesson wholly absorbed,
I am the elderly watching my youthfulness in the play of a child,
I am One with all: past, present and future.

4.9.2011

When the ordinary becomes miraculous ...

26

When the ordinary becomes miraculous, the miraculous becomes ordinary.

4.13.2011
Life begins with a breath …

27

Life begins with a breath in and ends with a breath out.
From the moment of birth until the moment of death, our
     breathing continues.
When we awake,
When we sleep,
When we walk,
When we run,
When we sit,
When we eat,
When we drink,
Breath plays the background music of our life.

How much time have you spent getting to know this life-giving force?
Have you played in the circle of breath? Have you felt it? Have you
experienced it?

The thread of air pulled in from beyond slowly fills our bodies, then
with a ribbon-like turn becomes the exhale that carries out the old and
releases it into the outer,

A quiet pause … silence … stillness … peace … bliss … .

As gently as we were placed in the world beyond breath, we are pulled
into the circle once again, pulling in the atmosphere that surrounds—
never thought about, always there.

(continued on the next page …)

4.13.2011
Life begins with a breath in ...

27 *(… continued)*

Our body knows breath as the seed knows growth and the flower knows to bloom. Breath is the intelligence of the Universe at work inside of us.

We do not breathe, we are breathed. Could we learn from watching this magical force breathing our bodies? Could we observe evolution unfolding? Could we become aware?

Listen to the music, dance to the rhythm!
Breath plays the music of life!

5.4.2011

Just as the water washes the stone smooth ...

28

Just as the water washes the stone smooth,
You can remain rigid like rock and become worn down over time,
Or fluid like water and remain forever changing yet forever the same—
In formless form.

5.11.2011
The most valuable thing …

29

The most valuable thing I can teach you is to forget what you have learned.

5.11.2011

I just point out what you already know ...

30

I just point out what you already know—true learning comes from within.

5.15.2011

The love we experience as a child ...

31

The love we experience as a child stays with us forever.
The love of a parent's warm hug,
The love of the shade of a tree,
The love of the smell of spring,
The love of the freedom of summer,
The love of the crackle of a fire,
The love of a day in the snow,
The love of our first kiss,
The love of our independence.
The love we experience as a child is the love we search for later.

It's always there.

Innocence has to be regained.
Complexity robs life of its treasure;
Simplicity returns us to love.

5.19.2011
I stare at the Moon ...

32

I stare at the Moon and feel it inside;
The quiet silence of presences resides,
Heavily at my core; the moonbeam connects,
The universal oneness, but my mind projects.
This is an object, not you-split;
I chuckle, my mind will never get it.
There is no object, only me;
The moon IS my soul, it's simple to see.
It's always present, yet not always seen;
It shines when darkness surrounds its gleam.
It reflects the light of Source that's too bright,
To look upon directly without losing sight.
I'm not in the Universe:
The Universe is me.
So hard to comprehend, so easy to see,
The Sun my Crown,
The Moon my Soul,
My body-The Universe-is only One: Whole.

5.24.2011

What we need as humanity ...

33

What we need as humanity is to spend time within. Spend time with the Whole. Spend time with the One that is all of us.

We are not bodies, we are the force of evolution that drives the physical beings that we are currently embodying. We are the Whole. But the only way we can figure this out is through our Self.

As with every opposite, when it is taken far enough, it comes back together to make the Whole. When you go deeply into yourself, you find the whole of humanity.

5.27.2011
Life is a dance …

34

Life is a dance, not a march.
You have to be fluid and feel it in your heart,
Not rigid dwelling in your mind.
You must embrace the moment—absorbing its beauty—
Not calculating where you are and where you are going to end up.

5.31.2011

You must wholly accept who you are ...

35

You must wholly accept who you are, which is total and complete glory. You can only find this truth after looking through all that you think you are now. You cannot transcend your thoughts by shutting them out or locking them in a dark closet in your mind. They must be exposed, examined and acknowledged for what they are—constructs of your mind.

Bring out your deepest worries, secrets and pains. Bring them out in front of you, place them on display and let them march in front of the greatness of your being. Watch them melt in the light. Use your microscope of meditation to examine them and realize they are nothing but space. They are not real. You only make them real by continuing to believe in them. You keep them locked away as bad or swirling about as worry. YOU give them energy.

Be aware, sit quietly and wait for these doors to open. Watch these forms of your mind come out of their hiding places. They will creep out and whisper in your ear,
"What about me?"
"Did you forget about this?"
"Who are you to sit here doing nothing, basking in the glory of light?"
"Come with me back to the cave of your mind where we live
       in darkness."
"You are wasting precious time! We must go back to the darkness so
       we can figure this out?"
"You can't accomplish anything here!"

(continued on the next page …)

5.31.2011

You must wholly accept who you are ...

35 *(… continued)*

Don't listen to the desperate claims of the dying ego! Remain in the light; do not return until the light has melted these illusions and you see clearly. Accept them as part of you, you made them! Don't push them back saying this is not me! It is the you that you have created, but not the you that is Whole.

Laugh at the pettiness of all your worries. Absorb them and become the light that showers your body. Look at how puny they appear in front of the Whole.

Bask in the greatness that is your glory!
Bask in the greatness that is your soul!

6.6.2011

Shadows dance beneath the trees …

36

Shadows dance beneath the trees as the summer wind wrestles through
their leaves.
Birds sing a tune while a caterpillar crawls across a green leaf
having lunch.
Geese float across the pond as if hand-in-hand, and turtles sunbathe on
the banks.

None seemed worried about yesterday or tomorrow, at peace with
themselves and the universe,
Not wondering who they are or what they will become,
Not wanting to be any more than they are at this very moment.

6.8.2011

When we are born into this world ...

37

When we are born into this world, we know everything that's important. We know how to love and how to be. We live in the moment looking at everything for what it is without the background noise of thought and judgment. We exist at peace with the universe, not expecting any more or less than we have right now. We are connected with the source that created us.

6.14.2011

Nothing that you are searching for is out there ...

38

Nothing that you are searching for is out there;
Everything you desire you already possess.
You must uncover and discover from within.

6.14.2011

Expansion, evolution, movement, desire …

39

Expansion, evolution, movement, desire:
These are the forces of the universe.
Nothing is at rest.

When you rest your body and create space in your mind,
You embody the forces of the universe.

The universal intelligence enters your mind.
You feel expansion, evolution, movement and desire on the
    cosmic level.
You become aligned with the powerful forces that move
    heavenly bodies,
Instead of opposing those forces as a single human.

Life flows like light filling a dark room.
Instant fulfillment!

6.16.2011

I watch my son looking at me …

40

I watch my son looking at me, inspecting my body as he feels my face with his hands–looking, feeling, inspecting–the eyes, nose, mouth, teeth, tongue and ears. As he explores, I gaze deep into his big blue eyes that are fixed on every detail. He savors every moment with no distraction. No thoughts running through his mind, no judgment; just pure love, joy and amazement at the form of the human body.

Then it hits me as the clutter that fills the background of my mind–bills need paying … , what do they think of this … , what will I do if … –breaks for just long enough for me to realize that I am looking at … *myself!* My son and I connect on a level beyond the grips of space and time! We explore each other! I am he and he is me!

I created him so that I could look at myself as a Whole, from a slight distance, just outside of my body. I created him so I could look at myself through the eyes of God–without judgment or expectations, without the background noise of self doubt. Seeing me with full potential, with pure love and admiration, with complete faith, he knows that I will be here when he needs me. Complete faith! Faith that I know best and will make sure that everything turns out perfectly. If only I still had faith like this … , but I do! For I am he and he is me and we are both all there is and all that will ever be! I didn't lose faith, I just lost *me!*

My son created me for many of the same reasons. He wanted to look at himself fresh from the side of spirit. He wanted to see unconditional love. He wanted to see that worldly things have no meaning when it comes to love. He wanted to experience the melting of the hardness of developing an ego. He wanted to show me the perfectness that I was as a child.

(continued on the next page …)

6.16.2011

I watch my son looking at me …

40 (... *continued)*

He wanted to let me know that I am still that perfection at my core. He wanted to explore himself through his father's eyes as I explored myself through my son's. God wanted to take a look at himself today in human form. For God is the Father, and the Son, that is I.

6.24.2011

The fingers of thought …

41

The fingers of thought,
Held together with the glue of time,
Rest upon our head.
Holding the energy of our local body down,
Shielding out the light of the eternal.
Separation …

As we sit, our thoughts gently release their grip,
One finger at a time,
As we slip into the gaps.
Closing fast their grip, we re-emerge into the life of constant thought.
But as we continue to return to this place,
Continue to quiet our minds,
Slowly …

The hands of time and fingers of thought gently loosen their grip.
The light from above shines down,
The energy from our body smokes up,
The eternal and local dance and mingle in the gaps.
The local becomes eternal as space and time melt away.
God is born in human form,
One becomes All and All becomes One.

6.24.2011

A situation outside of you …

42

A situation outside of you cannot cause a situation inside of you.
It's not possible.
Your interpretation of what happens outside triggers your
    inside response.
Events cannot cause stress.
Stress is caused by you, by your interpretation.
You have the power to control.
You cause stress,
Not your environment.
A relationship is not stressful,
Your interpretation is.
Work is not stressful,
Your interpretation is.
Your environment is not stressful,
Your mind is.

6.26.2011
The Universe spins above my head …

43

The Universe spins above my head;
Voices talk to me as faces appear.
Of them, my mind knows not.
The local has become nonlocal.
The same energy that moves planets beats my heart.
The same spirit that lives within me lives within all.
The vortex of life spins on every level.

6.27.2011

The person you have dreamed of becoming …

44

The person you have dreamed of becoming,
You have been all along.
You just need permission to unleash your inner greatness.
I give you that permission!
I will walk beside you for support!
A life of peace and joy is here at this very moment,
Waiting for you to accept it.

Release the negative thoughts that have run through your mind
    for years.
Release the pain that you hold onto.
You are the only one suffering.
You cause no pain except to yourself,
No one else can cause you pain.
You only hurt yourself by your interpretations of the world
    around you.
No external factor can penetrate within you without an invitation.

Let go of all that you have created in your mind,
BE that which you are:
The human manifestation of the Universe in all its glory.

6.27.2011
Everything is a tease ...

45

Everything is a tease with the mind;
A means to an end to get to the next step.
The stairs of thoughts never end,
Happiness is always promised on the next step;
Never found in the present.
Beyond The Mind is where happiness exists.
Right now, where you are, beyond your thoughts.
Heaven is not somewhere you go,
Happiness is not something to achieve,
Tomorrow you will not be happier than today!
Whatever the next step is, it will not give you what you want.
What you want you already have;
Heaven is available to you right now.
Move beyond mind,
Awaken to the Kingdom of Heaven!

The only thing holding you back is your mind—movement toward the next goal in anticipation of happiness.

6.29.2011

My body feels heavy …

46

My body feels heavy as my spirit sheds its skin.
The rush of unboundedness makes me dizzy.

I rush back to my thoughts,
Clinging to them like a light pole in the storm,
Trying to keep from being sucked from my earth body
And melting into Union.

The path is made; the door opened.

7.1.2011

Separateness ...

47

Separateness-
Body implies
Mind justifies
Soul defies

Unity-
I am you and you are I
Together we are God

7.6.2011
Uncertainty …

48

Uncertainty.
The mother of creation,
The father of opportunity,
All new arises out of uncertainty.

Why do we spend so much of our energy avoiding the very thing that allows us to evolve?

We must remain centered during uncertainty.

Refusing to be pulled to the surface, we remain present and centered as creation presents the opportunity to evolve. This centered, present awareness while evolving brings fulfillment and joy.

7.8.2011

The past of life is just like a dream ...

49

The past of life is just like a dream, no more fixed. Life can be altered in the present, just as you can formulate past in present simultaneously in your dreams to bring the exact situation you want. In dreams you can become engrossed in a detail as the whole scene is changed by the timeless stage hands. When you emerge from your focus, you find yourself in a completely new environment that supports your last thought.

The trail of thoughts that lead you through the perceived present of dreams drags the past along with you as a supporting set, so you never turn around and find yourself in the setting of past thoughts. The setting has become that of the present.

The same with the present in life. The past is nothing more than your imagination disguised as your memory. Of course, you can't change "things" that happened in the past, but what are "things" except food for memories.

You might say this is a toy from my past, but that is not true. It's a toy of the present that reminds you of an experience in the perceived past. The toy is of the present, if still physically available. If not, then it is only a memory of the imagination in the present of the perceived past.

By deepening your understanding in the present, you morph your past into the exact stepping stones needed for the future you desire which is unfolding now in the present.

(continued on the next page ...)

7.8.2011

The past of life is just like a dream …

49 (… continued)

You can't see the future from the present, only the memories and imaginations of the past projected into a future-like setting. The future unfolds as the present, just as the past. Therefore, you have control over both right now.

The flexibility of dreams and life are only different in your perception of the pliability and rigidness of each.

7.9.2011

We are here to experience the Whole …

50

We are here to experience the Whole through the five senses.
We are the Universe exploring itself as a human. Without our senses,
the universe does not exist as we know it. It is just waves of
energy: possibilities.

Our consciousness through our senses collapses the possibilities into
the universe we create.

There is no beauty until it is observed.
There is no music until it is heard.
There is no sweetness until it is tasted.
There is no smoothness until it is felt.
There is no fragrance until it is smelt.
There is only love without a body.

Our senses are our tools to create. We are not our senses; we are the
experience that flows through them. We create our human form to
experience ourselves just as the father creates a son.

We separate from the Whole to experience the Whole in form, but we
must not forget our source.

7.27.2011

We have many voices inside our heads …

51

We have many voices inside our heads. Most of us just know one, the one that drowns out the others. The one we think of as ourselves. As we sit, we slowly detach from this voice, realizing it is not us. It is our ego telling us all of our restrictions—reinforcing our limitations.

Our ego's voice tells us who we are from the ego's perspective. I must act like this ... and do this ... and say this ... We think that this is thinking, but it is our ego making sure we don't forget our tiny limited roles. Once this voice takes a break for a second or two, you get a small glimpse of the real you—expansive, whole, indefinable, powerful, beautiful, all knowing.

When you first tap this you, the one that is always there patiently waiting in the background, you will feel orgasmic. And you should. You are joining the Creator.

Over time you notice the main voice of the ego begins to break apart. It breaks into smaller and soft voices. It's now like being in a marketplace and overhearing all the conversations. You hear some of the strangest things being said. You hear family members and friends from past and present. You hear people that you have never met nor seen. As you go further, these voices quiet and you experience the Whole—clarity, creation, indivisible, eternal—God—You!

7.27.2011

There is no wonder why ...

52

There is no wonder why humanity is so confused.
Most of us don't find time to discover our voice,
We just repeat the voices in our head.

7.28.2011

Our consciousness expressed …

53

Our consciousness expressed through our five senses collapses the Universal fabric of pure potential into the reality we perceive.

Our collective consciousness creates our collective reality.

7.29.2011

Light is more beautiful …

54

Light is more beautiful making shadows through the trees.
The sky is more beautiful with some clouds.
You have had the experiences you have in life to offset the beauty you
    have become.
Contrast shows the true beauty of your light.

7.31.2011

Love is the field of Unity ...

55

Love is the field of Unity;
We arise from love and fall back to love.
Our separateness is forgetting this fact,
Our attempt to protect ourselves as we forget who we are.
Remember love,
Return to love,
Be,
Love.

7.31.2011

Meditation can't be described in words ...

56

Meditation can't be described in words;
It is the space between words.
The words merely point to the silence between them.

8.1.2011

Judgment is the ego talking ...

57

Judgment is the ego talking.

It's not your voice, it's the voice in your head.

When the ego judges, it reminds you of the petty.

It seeks to justify the limited role that the ego constricts you to.

Judgment keeps you from being your expanded powerful self.

It reduces you to the limited self you perceive that you are when you
    live life under the false protection of the ego.

The ego judges others as a way to define itself.

This creates separateness.

This creates weakness.

Without judgment we become our true self.

Whole.

Powerful.

Loving.

8.1.2011

The center of the Universe is not a planet ...

58

The center of the Universe is not a planet, galaxy or star, but consciousness. From Consciousness all matter arises.

8.2.2011

Be out to give ...

59

Be out to give, not out to get, and you will get what you give. Love.

8.2.2011

If it can be taken away …

60

If it can be taken away by someone other than you, it is not real and, therefore, not important.

8.2.2011

The chatter in your head ...

61

The chatter in your head is the fog on the mirror. You can't see yourself clearly unless you wipe it clean. When it is wiped clean, you will see your true undistorted beauty.

8.4.2011

Humanity faces challenges ...

62

Humanity faces challenges because too many people are trying to be who they think they should be rather than being who they are.

Discover yourself and blossom,
Unite with your true purpose,
Suppression is separation,
Separation is weakness.

Be whole,
Be powerful,
Be the human expression of the Universe,
Be the human expression of God.

8.4.2011

When you merge . . .

63

When you merge with God, you see God everywhere in everything. When something is everywhere in everything, it disappears. It is separate no more. When you see God in everyone and everything, you have a deep love for it all. God then disappears into Unity with you, and only Love is left. Everything merges into Love, and there is nothing separate.

8.4.2011

How does a flower know when to bloom …

64

How does a flower know when to bloom?
How does a tree know when to bud?
How does the tide know when to change?
How does the sun know when to rise?
How does the seed know when to sprout?
How does the child know when to be born?

Why do we think we know more than the Universe?
Why do we think we can control with our ego?

8.8.2011

Following your heart makes you happy …

65

Following your heart makes you happy. Denying your heart because it doesn't make sense to your mind makes you unhappy. Your mind is your tool to help you follow your heart. You heart is your tool for letting you know when your mind has led you astray.

8.8.2011

In stillness there is movement ...

66

In stillness there is movement,
In silence there is music,
God is everywhere; God is nowhere.
You become centered and the center disappears.
You become Whole: full and empty.

8.8.2011

Can you change the past ...

67

Can you change the past?

The past is just as fluid as the future. The past is a memory, and the future is a fantasy. Both are your imagination.

So how can we change the past? Since your past is just a memory, then it is up to you to decide what that memory is. Have you ever had something happen, and at first you thought it was "bad," but after time passed, you find that it was something that was very beneficial for your life? Did the past not change?

The event that happened did not change, but your interpretation of it did. Since the past is just a memory, then your interpretation is all that matters.

8.9.2011
Who are you …

68

Who are you? Who are you when you don't answer with your name? Who are you when you don't answer with the roles that you play such as mother, doctor or artist? Who are you when you don't allow your mind to repeat what society says about you? Who are you when you escape the limitations these labels inherently imply? Who are you when you feel the answer? Who are you?

8.10.2011
My cells tingle as stars twinkle ...

69

My cells tingle as stars twinkle; I connect with the Universe within.

8.15.2011

To be free from fear …

70

To be free from fear is to not be fearful of fear.
To have certainty is to embrace uncertainty.
To have clarity is to realize you can only see within.
To have confidence is to dissolve the ego.
Nothing is timeless in time;
Timeless freedom, certainty, clarity and confidence arise from the truth
within you.
All opposites melt in the glory of the Divine.

8.15.2001

Silence means more than words …

71

Silence means more than words;
Stillness accomplishes more than action.
Emptiness fills you,
And life is fulfilled.

8.16.2011

You do not have to wait …

72

You do not have to wait until you die to experience heaven or hell;
You have both available to you today.
If you use your mind as a tool, you are in heaven.
If your mind uses you as a tool, you are in hell.

8.16.2011

To judge is to stifle creativity …

73

To judge is to stifle creativity,
To judge is to add a period. in the middle of a sentence.

Labeling what happens reduces it to the result,
A false result that we are declaring as now.
The result is not here yet;
The present flows into eternity.

Why declare this moment the end with your judgment?
Why collapse down the possibilities of life with your mind?
Why create a false ending?

Observe the flow of life in its glory,
Miraculous in every moment.
Always destroying old to create new,
Never good or bad,
Just flowing.

Creation, evolution, expansion—flowing.

8.18.2011
Anger should not be suppressed ...

74

Anger should not be suppressed.
It is a key to the depths of our being.
It should be accepted as a gift.
Feel it bubble to the surface,
Feel its heat or chill,
Watch your ego churn in the emotion.
Stay centered as the observer;
Let anger run its course.
Don't project your anger on others,
It has nothing to do with them.
Be selfish, stay centered, and watch it dissolve.
Suppression builds up pressure;
Dissolution resolves.

8.20.2011

The material world is the creation ...

75

The material world is the creation of our senses.
The outside world does not exist outside,
It exists inside the human.
A tree is only a tree inside of us.
It's only a tree at the level of the human senses.
Science tells us it is a swirl of electrons,
Mostly space;
The tree only exists when we direct our consciousness to it.
Its beauty is our beauty,
Everything arises from within.

8.22.2011

Clarity is a feeling ...

76

Clarity is a feeling, not a mental state.
It's a break from mental–mind.
The mind stops, and clarity arises;
It is always there, yet obscured by noise.

When clarity breaks like the dawn of a new day,
it sheds its light upon the world:
Your light!
And your light is reflected back upon you by every object in existence.
The world transforms in an instant, from the mundane and ordinary to
the miraculous and extraordinary.

Clarity exposes the dance of life,
The fabric of being,
The love of light.

The night has ceased to exist and has given birth to a new awareness.
Look around at the beauty of sight,
Rejoice that you can now see,
Be one with the object so your separation melts,
Join in clarity with all things.

8.23.2011

Destruction is creation …

77

Destruction is creation in its infancy.
Destruction clears the path providing access to the fertile ground that lies just beneath the surface.
Destruction wipes the slate clean, canceling out all that we have built in vain so that we can begin anew today with our newly enriched perspective.
Destruction forces us to give up on the fruitless projects we have constructed, so we may follow our heart down the new path.
Destruction is a release: the release of built up energy, the release of suppression so it can bloom into creation.
Destruction is creation in its infancy,
Eternal the cycle.

8.24.2011

This life is no different than a dream …

78

This life is no different than a dream.
When you are having a dream, you feel like it is real,
You feel like everything is happening to you.
Then you wake up and realize it was all in your mind.

When you awaken to this life, you realize the same thing,
It's all in your head.

8.25.2011

The melting of the ego is the path …

79

The melting of the ego is the path to true confidence.
The facade of confidence is the ego being defensive,
Assuring you and the world that you are the powerful person you think
you should be.

This is confidence inspired by fear.
There is always a shadow to anything fear induced.
Running from fear separates you from your soul.
You, on the level of your soul, have nothing to fear.
This is true confidence,
Inspired by peace and love.

Melt the ego that traps and limits you,
Unleash the greatness that is you,
Bask in the peace of confident living,
The Universe embraces Soulful existence.

8.26.2011

Desire fades as you merge …

80

Desire fades as you merge into the Whole.
How could you *want* when you *are*?
How can you desire when you are fulfilled?
You are that which you desire;
Your perceived separateness creates an illusion that you must seek.
Realize.

8.27.2011

Happiness is the origin …

81

Happiness is the origin, not a result.
Happiness begins with you and extends to your outside world.
Nothing outside of you can make you truly happy.
True happiness is always there, you just have to uncover it.
The false happiness situations and material things bring is quickly
    replaced when the next desire arises.
When you are joyful, all things bring happiness.
When you search for happiness outside yourself, joy is never found.
Happiness is the origin;
Love.

8.29.2011

Meditation is the planting ...

82

Meditation is the planting of the seed.
Action is harvesting the crops.
If you meditate and take no action,
Your food will rot in the field and be of no use to you.
If you only take action without meditation,
You will be harvesting weeds.

8.29.2011
The ancient womb …

83

The ancient womb of the warm Atlantic engulfs me as the light from the sun tingles my cells down to my core.
Kaleidoscopic colors rotate before my closed eyes.
Waves of peace and love gently wash over my body.
My mind stops to feel the Whole;
I'm floating in the sea of possibility.

8.30.2011

We have two choices …

84

We have two choices:
Allow the flow of life to unfold with awareness.
Constrict the flow of life by becoming more rigid.
The dam is broken.

8.30.2011

To be present …

85

To be present
To be love
To be light

9.1.2011

You cannot remain changeless …

86

You cannot remain changeless;
You are either expanding or contracting.
Expansion is your natural flow.
Centered, one approaches changelessness.
You are like water:
Forever in formless form.

9.2.2011

If you don't know yourself ...

87

If you don't know yourself, you can't know anything about the
  outside world.

The outside world arises in you,
It is seen through the filter of your mind.

You don't see what really exists;
You see your thoughts projected:
You see yourself.

If you are not getting what you want on the outside,
The only place to look is inside.

9.2.2011

Clarity comes from clearing …

88

Clarity comes from clearing out all your preconceptions:
The fog is within.
Situations don't obscure clarity—your predetermined reactions do.

9.5.2011

We drown among our possessions …

89

We drown among our possessions. The more things we have, the more of our time is consumed caring for and keeping them. Life is suffocated by the material. The surface becomes our focus, and the center cannot be found.

9.5.2011

It's not what I teach …

90

It's not what I teach that's important;
It's what you learn.

You will learn more from developing awareness than from
    the specifics.
The fact that I teach you to do "this" is not as important as you
    recognizing what you do now which may currently go unnoticed.

Doing unconsciously is sleep walking,
Being conscious is life,
Observe.

9.5.2011

What you seek is within …

91

What you seek is within,
However, this does not mean that there is no journey.
Throughout the journey you must keep your focus at your core:
Remain centered.

Everything you see along the way will be a reflection of yourself.
This reflection points to your true self.
Go within.

9.10.2011

Just as the rocks ...

92

Just as the rocks in the river show us the movement of the current,
So do the obstacles of our lives show us the flow of our destiny.
The rocks teach us about the river:
Marking clear the path of movement,
Revealing the speed of the current.

The obstacles in our lives teach us about our Self.

The water does not try to move rocks;
It simply flows around them without resistance,
Changing form without hesitation,
Flowing.

9.10.2011

Personal Growth is what matters …

93

Personal Growth is what matters,
Obtaining a deeper understanding of who you are,
What you want, and why you are here.

Find who you are and every aspect of life will flourish;
Ignore who you are and any type of growth will be short lived:
Unsustainable.

9.12.2011

Meditation gives you clarity …

94

Meditation gives you clarity and comfort in uncertainty. Everything is always evolving, therefore, you must know who you are to know how to respond. If you go through life copying others, you will never know peace and happiness.

You must find your own way to create the masterpiece that is life. A child enjoys painting by the numbers because he gets quick results that look as he thinks things should. Few adults find pleasure in painting by numbers.

The results aren't what matters. How you get the results determines your happiness. You must be authentic and come from within.

9.13.2011
We must observe ...

95

We must observe feelings, emotions and intuition as they arise and fall.
Not suppressing and not projecting but observing them within,
Observing their origin,
Observing the lessons they are teaching about the Self:
Acting from awareness.

9.14.2011

We are the waves …

96

We are the waves arising from the ocean of God,
Separate only on the surface,
Arising from the Whole.

9.18.2011

Freedom is saying what you believe ...

97

Freedom is saying what you believe,
Knowing yourself,
Trusting your heart,
Living from the soul,
Being,
Free.

9.19.2011

Life is not the surface …

98

Life is not the surface;
Every experience holds a key to your soul.
It's not what happens in life, but what you learn.
Every event has a hidden lesson for the Self.
Awakening to those lessons is the purpose of life:
To know yourself.

Nothing happens outside of you.

9.20.2011

Life is a circle …

99

Life is a circle.
All paths on the surface of life lead to the beginning.
The true path is to your core.
The destination of the journey is not important;
It's what you learn about yourself along the way.

9.20.2011

You are the force of the Universe ...

100

You are the force of the Universe expressing itself in human form.
You are beyond fear and worry.
You are Spirit just as the waves are the ocean–
Only appearing separate on the surface–
Comingling eternally in the depths.
To keep the charge you must bathe yourself in the space beyond mind.

9.26.2011

Walking around in a slumber ...

101

Walking around in a slumber, we pass each and every day,
Looking for a pointer or a sign along the way.
We rise from bed in the morning, only to retire later on;
We leave to go to work and return home when done.
We fill our cup with tea, and then it is gone;
We fill our mind with thoughts and then move beyond.
The surface of life ends, exactly where it begins.
Nothing is gained or lost,
Except from within.

9.30.2011

Freedom cannot arise from fear ...

102

Freedom cannot arise from fear;
The Whole cannot be found by separating:
Unconditional love for all.

10.2.2011

Understanding who you are ...

103

Understanding who you are is the most worthy intention.
This wisdom is the foundation for all action.
You act to meet false needs if you only see the surface;
This produces a life of struggle.
The only struggle in life is the struggle you create by assuming a
    false self,
A self that is separate from the Whole.

10.3.2011

The deeper you dig …

104

The deeper you dig,
The farther you see.
Silence teaches more
Than words could ever teach.

Words point into
The depth of silence beneath.
To understand words,
You must experience and be.

The words are just a trick,
An artificial lure,
To take you beyond contradiction,
To the space that is your core;

The space from which you arise,
The space for which you search,
The space that you are,
The space beyond this earth.

Move past the language of men,
Become the Divine within.

10.3.2011

Everything is dark until …

105

Everything is dark until light shines upon it.
It was not absent when it was dark,
It just could not be seen.
Let the eternal light shine through you,
Light up your life so you can see and be seen.

10.4.2011

This moment in time lasts forever ...

106

This moment in time lasts forever.
It existed before you were born in human form and will continue after
    the body's death.
There is no past or future, only this moment.
You are outside of time.
Time does not pass,
Forms grow old and decay.
The circle of life continues;
You are eternal.

10.7.2011

You are just a vessel …

107

You are just a vessel for the love of God to flow through.
Your past experience means nothing.
Your worldly qualifications have no value in the space of the Supreme.
The ability to tap into and become the infinite is your gift.
This is true knowledge.
In this space, you are all knowing and free,
Open to the flow of love, beauty and peace,
Open to the flow of the Cosmos that is you.

10.8.2011

Love unites all causes ...

108

Love unites all causes;
Even hate and anger arise from a need to be loved.
Go and unite the Separate:
Love.

10.10.2011

The society we have created ...

109

The society we have created based on fear and taking from one another
  has failed.
We must shift to love,
We must care for each other,
For *we* are not *we* at all:
One.

10.15.2011

Meditation is not religion …

110

Meditation is not religion;
Meditation is your base.
Meditation is spirituality,
A place beneath face.

Meditation is sexual.
Meditation is grace.
Meditation will take you farther,
No time; no space.

Meditation is powerful
In a useful way.
Meditation takes you to a world:
No work, all play.

Meditation is transformational,
Find your Soul along the way.
Meditation is finding out
That you are God today.

Meditation takes you to a place
Where we are all One.
The place we began,
Where we return when done.

Meditation takes you to your core
So you know who you are:
The Divine Light shining
Through You who are the Star.

10.18.2011

When you have no fear ...

111

When you have no fear,
You have complete freedom.
Your fears are your master;
They keep you in chains.
Knowing the truth breaks all chains:
You are the chains.

One, Whole, Love–Divine

10.21.2011
The mind is a wonderful servant …

112

The soul is a master;
The mind is a servant.
Allow the glory of the divine to flow,
Melt the fear that is your mind.

10.25.2011
The creation of the body begins …

113

The creation of the body begins with the seed of the soul,
A circle,
Whole and eternal,
Nothing yet everything,
From that which we arise we fall,
A wave traveling through the ocean of eternity.

10.25.2011
Reality is fluid …

114

Reality is fluid perception, not rigid material.

11.4.2011
Embracing detachment …

115

Embracing detachment, you automatically free yourself
     from suppression.
Suppression is acting against your will because of your attachment to a
     certain result.
Suppression causes pain.
Suppression separates you:
From who you are,
From your core,
From your soul.

11.9.2011

The deeper you go ...

116

The deeper you go, the more perspective you have.
Just as scientists find infinity looking in between stars and electrons,
You find infinity in the potential of consciousness
And the beauty of the world the senses create.

11.10.2011

Everything we see ...

117

Everything we see is a reflection of ourselves.
When we see anything other than divine light in physical form,
We are forgetting our essence.
We are allowing the ego's judgment to define us,
Therefore, a perceived object.
Any judgment we place on an object has grown from a limitation we
    place on ourselves.

The pond is only water, the reflection we see is our own.

About The Author

Kyle P. Harper writes, teaches and advises. He has appeared on NPR, CBS and Fox and been featured in major newspapers and magazines talking about his experiences. In addition to his writings, you can hear about his journey and experience the meditation techniques he uses in workshops and retreats.

For more information, visit www.kylepharper.com or www.movingbeyondmind.com.